SPORTS GREAT GREG MADDUX

—*Sports Great Books*—

BASEBALL

Sports Great Jim Abbott
0-89490-395-0/ Savage
Sports Great Barry Bonds
0-89490-595-3/ Sullivan
Sports Great Bobby Bonilla
0-89490-417-5/ Knapp
Sports Great Roger Clemens
0-89490-284-9/ Devaney
Sports Great Orel Hershiser
0-89490-389-6/ Knapp
Sports Great Bo Jackson
0-89490-281-4/ Knapp
Sports Great Greg Maddux
0-89490-873-1/ Thornley
Sports Great Kirby Puckett
0-89490-392-6/ Aaseng
Sports Great Cal Ripken, Jr.
0-89490-387-X/ Macnow
Sports Great Nolan Ryan
0-89490-394-2/ Lace
Sports Great Darryl Strawberry
0-89490-291-1/ Torres & Sullivan

BASKETBALL

Sports Great Charles Barkley
0-89490-386-1/ Macnow
Sports Great Larry Bird
0-89490-368-3/ Kavanagh
Sports Great Muggsy Bogues
0-89490-876-6/ Rekela
Sports Great Patrick Ewing
0-89490-369-1/ Kavanagh
Sports Great Anfernee Hardaway
0-89490-758-1/ Rekela
Sports Great Magic Johnson (Revised and Expanded)
0-89490-348-9/ Haskins
Sports Great Michael Jordan
0-89490-370-5/ Aaseng
Sports Great Karl Malone
0-89490-599-6/ Savage
Sports Great Reggie Miller
0-89490-874-X/ Thornley
Sports Great Alonzo Mourning
0-89490-875-8/ Fortunato
Sports Great Hakeem Olajuwon
0-89490-372-1/ Knapp
Sports Great Shaquille O'Neal
0-89490-594-5/ Sullivan
Sports Great Scottie Pippen
0-89490-755-7/ Bjarkman
Sports Great David Robinson
0-89490-373-X/ Aaseng
Sports Great Dennis Rodman
0-89490-759-X/ Thornley
Sports Great John Stockton
0-89490-598-8/ Aaseng
Sports Great Isiah Thomas
0-89490-374-8/ Knapp
Sports Great Dominique Wilkins
0-89490-754-9/ Bjarkman

FOOTBALL

Sports Great Troy Aikman
0-89490-593-7/ Macnow
Sports Great John Elway
0-89490-282-2/ Fox
Sports Great Jim Kelly
0-89490-670-4/ Harrington
Sports Great Joe Montana
0-89490-371-3/ Kavanagh
Sports Great Jerry Rice
0-89490-419-1/ Dickey
Sports Great Barry Sanders
0-89490-418-3/ Knapp
Sports Great Herschel Walker
0-89490-207-5/ Benagh

HOCKEY

Sports Great Wayne Gretzky
0-89490-757-3/ Rappoport
Sports Great Mario Lemieux
0-89490-596-1/ Knapp

TENNIS

Sports Great Steffi Graf
0-89490-597-X/ Knapp
Sports Great Pete Sampras
0-89490-756-5/ Sherrow

SPORTS GREAT GREG MADDUX

Stew Thornley

—Sports Great Books—

Enslow Publishers, Inc.

44 Fadem Road
Box 699
Springfield, NJ 07081
USA

PO Box 38
Aldershot
Hants GU12 6BP
UK

Library of Congress Cataloging-in-Publication Data

Thornley, Stew.
Sports great Greg Maddux / Stew Thornley.
p. cm. — (Sports great books)
Includes index.
Summary: A biography of the star pitcher for the Atlanta Braves who has won the Cy Young Award for four consecutive years.
ISBN 0-89490-873-1
1. Maddux, Greg, 1966– —Juvenile literature. 2. Baseball players—United States—Biography—Juvenile literature. 3. Pitchers (Baseball)—United States—Biography—Juvenile literature.
[1. Maddux, Greg, 1966– . 2. Baseball players.]
I. Title. II. Series.
GV865.M319T56 1997
796.357'092—dc20
[B]

95-49720
CIP
AC

Printed in the United States of America

10 9 8 7 6 5 4 3 2 1

Illustration Credits: Brenda L. Himrich, pp. 47, 50, 53; Linda McGowan, pp. 19, 20; Philadelphia Phillies, pp. 28, 44; Ron Vesely, pp. 9, 11, 13, 26, 33, 36, 38, 41, 59; Stew Thornley, p. 56; University of Arizona, p. 22.

Cover Photo: Ron Vesely

Contents

Chapter 1

Greg Maddux hopped out of a taxicab and walked into Mile High Stadium in Denver, Colorado. His team, the Atlanta Braves, would be playing the Colorado Rockies, and Maddux would be on the mound. Inside the stadium, Maddux went through his usual pregame routine.

But there would be nothing routine about this game. Even though it was only August 11, it looked like it might be the final game of the 1994 baseball season. Because of a labor dispute with the owners, it appeared that major-league players would go on strike the next day. No one was sure how long it would last and no one was happy about it, least of all Maddux.

He had been pitching well throughout the season but especially over the last few weeks. Many people had not noticed, though. The focus this year had been on hitting.

The 1994 season was one in which the hitters went wild. It was another reason people were sorry to see the season come to an early finish. Matt Williams of the San Francisco Giants had a chance of breaking Roger Maris's single-season home run record. Tony Gwynn of the San Diego Padres had a batting average of .394; fans were hoping he could raise it a few points and become the first player since 1941 to hit .400 in a season. But the chance for these great achievements would be wiped out if the season did not continue.

With the way the hitters had been cleaning up, it was tough for a pitcher to stand out. Another disadvantage Maddux faced is that his home ballpark, Atlanta-Fulton County Stadium, is considered a good place for hitters. The short distances to the fence in Atlanta's park make it an easy place to hit home runs. As a result, it has been nicknamed "The Launching Pad." Maddux pitches approximately half his games in the Launching Pad. And in this game he would be pitching in Mile High Stadium, well known as another graveyard for pitchers.

Despite all of this, Maddux had been having one of the greatest seasons a pitcher has ever had. Coming into the game against the Rockies, he had an earned run average (ERA) of 1.63. An ERA indicates how many earned runs (runs not scored as a result of errors made by the fielders) a pitcher gives up every nine innings. Usually, an ERA of under 3.50 is considered good. In this Year of the Hitter, though, an ERA of 3.50 would be outstanding. Maddux's earned run average, less than half of that, was truly phenomenal.

By the time Maddux took the mound in the bottom of the first inning in Colorado, the Braves already had a 1–0 lead. As it turned out, that was all Maddux needed. The Atlanta hitters, however, went on to score many more. It was as though they knew this would be the last chance to flex their muscles this season. Even Maddux got into the act. He had 3 hits and drove in 2 of the Braves' 13 runs in the game.

Maddux gave up an infield hit to Gerald Young leading off the game for Colorado. Young was caught stealing, though. Maddux retired the next two batters and was on a roll.

Going into the game against the Colorado Rockies, Greg Maddux had an outstanding 1.63 earned run average.

With two out in the third, pinch hitter Trenidad Hubbard reached base on an error. But Maddux ended the inning by snaring a ground ball Young hit back at him and threw him out at first. There would be no more base runners for the Rockies until the eighth inning.

Through the middle innings Maddux was flawless. Not only did he retire every batter he faced, his control was perfect. When he started off Walt Weiss with a pitch outside the strike zone in the seventh, it was the first ball he had thrown since the fourth inning.

Weiss then hit a grounder to first baseman Fred McGriff. For the third time in the game, Maddux raced over to cover first as McGriff flipped the ball to him for the out. Maddux also managed to react and catch a wicked line drive hit by

Mike Kingery two innings before. Like his pitching this day, his play in the field was typical for him. Regarded as the best fielding pitcher in the National League, Maddux was on his way to winning his fifth straight Gold Glove.

Maddux gave up two infield singles with one out in the eighth but retired the next two batters to finish the inning. He put down the Rockies in order in the ninth to end the game—and the season. The next day the players' strike began, and baseball did not resume until the following spring.

For Maddux, both this game and the entire season had been terrific. In the game, he did not walk a batter and allowed just three infield hits, pitching his third shutout of the season. Not only that, the Rockies hit only two balls out of the infield all afternoon, both flies to Dave Gallagher in left field. Center fielder Mike Kelly and David Justice in right might as well have stayed in the dugout. Neither touched a ball on the field all day.

The win was Maddux's sixteenth victory of the season. It tied him with Ken Hill of the Montreal Expos for the league lead. But no one was even close to him in earned run average. The shutout in Colorado lowered his ERA to 1.56. This is a statistic any pitcher would be proud to have in any season. But what makes it all the better is that the ERA for the entire National League was 4.21. The difference of 2.65 runs per game between Maddux's ERA and the league average was the largest in the history of major-league baseball.

The pitcher in the majors with the next-best earned run average was Steve Ontiveros of the Oakland Athletics. His ERA was 2.65, over a run more a game than Maddux's. This difference was also a major-league record.

Why is Maddux so difficult to hit against? Hitters have wondered about that. As they stand in the on-deck circle, many have been eager to get up to the plate and face Maddux.

In a season when batters were hitting extremely well, Maddux had an ERA of 1.56. The National League average was 4.21—a difference of 2.65 runs per game.

He does not have an overpowering fastball and, from a distance, looks like he might be easy to hit against. But batters find out differently when they get into the batter's box.

Even though he is not likely to blow a fastball by a batter with sheer speed, Maddux's variety of pitches is awesome. His best pitch is actually his change-up. A change-up is nothing more than a slow pitch. It should be easy to wallop—if a hitter knows it is coming. But if a batter is expecting a harder pitch like a fastball or a slider, he can be left helpless when the pitcher fools him with a change-up. Maddux is a master at making hitters feel helpless. "I try to throw the pitch the hitter is least expecting," he says.

Maddux also benefits from having great control of his pitches. He is usually able to deliver the pitches to the exact location that he wants. He does not walk many batters. But it also means he can deliver pitches in the strike zone to spots where they are hard to hit, such as on the corners of the plate.

By mixing up his pitches, changing speeds and locations, Maddux makes the most of each of his pitches. Todd Benzinger of the San Francisco Giants once said of Maddux's fastball, "It's not the hardest fastball, but it is the best fastball as far as getting people out."

For Maddux, it is not a matter of being gifted with the greatest pitching arm ever. There is no question that he has been blessed with a great deal of athletic talent. In fact, this talent runs in the family. Maddux's older brother, Mike, also pitches in the major leagues. Although he has not achieved the same success as Greg, Mike has put together a nice career and has pitched for several different teams.

What makes Greg so outstanding is his ability to squeeze the most out of the talent he has. He is considered one of the smartest pitchers in the game. Maddux studies videotapes, not of his own pitching mechanics, but of opposing hitters. He

Maddux studies the hitters he pitches against. He learns their strengths and weaknesses, and pitches to the weaknesses.

gets to know their strengths and weaknesses—then he pitches to those weaknesses. His pitching coach with the Braves, Leo Mazzone, says, "He's well prepared for each game, and he's a great student of the game."

Being a good student pays off for Maddux. For his sensational 1994 performance, he received the National League's Cy Young Award as the best pitcher in the league. It was the third-straight year he won the award. This feat had never been accomplished before.

His three-hit shutout against the Rockies in the final game of the year was typical of his entire season. It was just about as good a game—and as good a season—as a pitcher could possibly have.

The early ending to the season because of the strike interrupted a lot of great performances. As baseball analyst Alan Holst points out, most sportswriters and fans zeroed in on what hitters like Matt Williams and Tony Gwynn might have done if not for the strike. "What few people noticed," Holst adds, "was the season Greg Maddux *did* have." In a great year for the hitters, he won the earned-run-average title by the greatest margin in history. Pitching in the best hitters' park in the league, his ERA was better, compared to the league average, than any previous single-season mark ever.

"Who knows, maybe Maddux would have fallen off had they played the entire season. Then again, maybe he would have just gotten better. What we do know is that he had a year that nobody ever had before. Remember it."

Chapter 2

Children with parents in the military tend to move around a lot. They learn to make new friends quickly as they travel from place to place. It is a different type of childhood from that of most kids, and they are sometimes affectionately called "army brats." For Greg Maddux and his older siblings, the term would more accurately be "air force brats."

Their father, Dave, served in the air force for twenty-two years. During that time, Dave and his wife, Linda, moved to different places around the country and the world, adding to their family as they went.

The oldest Maddux child, a daughter named Terri, was born in Anchorage, Alaska, when her father was stationed at Elmendorf Air Force Base in 1959. Two years later, the family was living in Dayton, Ohio, when a son, Mike, was born. Greg came along five years later. He was born on April 14, 1966, in San Angelo, Texas.

The military transfers continued, and the Maddux family never stayed in one place for too long. During the time of the Vietnam conflict, in the late 60s and early 70s, Dave received an assignment in Thailand. The rest of the family stayed in the United States. Linda packed up her kids and moved back to Decatur County in Indiana, where her parents were. The nearest major-league baseball team was in Cincinnati. Dave and Linda Maddux had been fans of the Reds when they were growing up. Now their children started with the same allegiance. Pete Rose, the Reds' great star, became a favorite of the Maddux family.

When Dave returned after a year overseas, the family was reunited. They were still on the move, however. After stops in Minot, North Dakota, and Riverside, California, Dave received another assignment overseas. This time, however, the family stayed together and, in January 1973, moved to Spain.

By this time, Greg was six years old and beginning to follow his sister and brother in athletic pursuits. "This was the most active time we had as far as the whole family being involved in sports," recalled Linda Maddux.

Greg and Mike played Little League baseball as well as football. In addition to softball, Terri took part in track and field. She was an excellent runner and, according to her parents, can still outrun her kid brothers to this day.

All three children participated in basketball. Greg and Mike especially loved the sport and played it for many years. It was apparent, however, that they were both extremely gifted when it came to baseball. After they got to high school, both Greg and Mike were urged by coaches to forget about basketball and focus on baseball.

Sports, especially baseball, seemed to be a way of life for the Maddux children in Spain. Linda remembers how Mike and Greg would play baseball all day out in the hot sun. "Then they'd get home and the first thing they'd do is head back outside to play more baseball in the hot sun. Finally, I came to the realization that they were doing what they wanted to do."

In pickup games on the sandlots, it was not unusual for Greg to join Mike and his friends, even though they were several years older. Even in organized leagues, Greg often found himself as one of the smallest players on the team. His birthday fell near the end of the cutoff day for his particular age group. As a result, most of the players on the team were older than he was.

Playing with and against older and bigger kids may have been beneficial to Greg, according to his father, who said, "He was always the littlest kid on the team, and he had to play harder to succeed. He was never intimidated by kids who were older or bigger than him. That's probably helped him."

Dave Maddux encouraged his children's interest in sports. Although Dave had grown up in Indiana, his favorite player when he was younger was Mickey Mantle of the New York Yankees. He never forgot what he learned while reading Mantle's autobiography. "He [Mantle] credited his father with making him what he was and, because of that, believed that ballplayers were not born but made. I promised myself then that if I ever had any boys, I'd put that theory to the test and see if it was true."

Dave spent as much time as he could in the backyard with both Mike and Greg, playing catch and hitting grounders to them. He also made them think about baseball. Dave constantly quizzed his sons on how they would respond in certain situations. "It's why we were always way ahead of the other kids our own age," says Mike. "By the time we played Little League, we were so sound in the basics, we didn't need to waste time learning them like the other kids. We just reacted."

Eventually, the Maddux family was able to settle down in one spot. Dave received an assignment at Nellis Air Force Base in Las Vegas, Nevada, in August 1976. Three years later, while still stationed at Nellis, Dave retired from the air force as a senior master sergeant. By this time the Maddux family had established roots. They liked Las Vegas and decided to stay there.

Since Nevada is a state in which gambling is legal, Las Vegas is a city known for its many casinos. Dave took advantage of that fact and got a job as a poker dealer after leaving the military. He has worked at a number of casinos through the years—including the Sahara Inn and the Excalibur. He now does his dealing at the MGM Grand Hotel on the Las Vegas Boulevard strip.

At the time Dave was going from the air force back to civilian life, his oldest two children were in college. Mike had just left to attend the University of Texas at El Paso on a baseball scholarship. Terri had stayed in town, having enrolled at the University of Nevada, Las Vegas. Meanwhile, Greg was on the verge of entering high school.

He would attend a different school than his sister and brother had, though. Terri and Mike had gone to Rancho High School, which was the school serving the area that included the air force base. When Dave left the military, his family had moved into another house in the southeast part of the city. The school that covered this area was Valley High School.

Maddux benefited by having the chance to play for an outstanding coach, Rodger Fairless, at Valley High. The team even won the state baseball championship during Maddux's junior season. Fairless remembers Maddux for more than just his great pitching. "He had a way about him that made you grin, that kept everyone loose," said Fairless, who added that it was Maddux's overall manner, not just a strong arm, that made him a star. "He had teammates who could throw harder than he could. The thing that always made Greg different was

After Greg's father retired from the air force, the Madduxes moved to this house in Las Vegas. The family no longer lives here.

his control and his poise. He pitched the same, no matter what the team and what the score."

Many baseball experts believe that one of the reasons that Maddux is so good today is that he never had a great fastball to start off with. Many young pitchers who can blow fastballs by just about every batter never actually learn how to pitch. Maddux never had that luxury. As a result, he had to learn to pitch right from the start.

Maddux learned a lot from Rodger Fairless. But he also picked up some lessons about pitching during Sunday afternoon workouts on the sandlots of Las Vegas. These workouts were overseen by Ralph Medar, a former major-league baseball scout, and Manny Guerrera, another baseball man who enjoyed working with kids. Guerrera spent his time giving hitting instruction while Medar concentrated on the pitchers. Just about anyone in the Las Vegas area who had hopes of playing professional baseball made it a point to attend these practices. Often players from the University of Nevada, Las Vegas, baseball team would stop by, both to get instruction from Medar and Guerrera and to help out with the younger players.

Maddux first went to these workouts while tagging around with Mike. It was not long, though, before he caught Medar's eye. One of the first things Medar taught Maddux was how to throw a change-up. "The change-up is not going to be a good pitch against high school hitters," Medar told him. "You could just throw your fastball and get most of them out, but down the line a good change-up is harder to hit than any pitch." Not only that, a change-up is a pitch that would put little stress on a still developing arm. Maddux was fourteen when he learned the pitch. At that age, many aspiring pitchers are trying to snap off curve balls or overpower hitters with blazing

Greg played baseball for Valley High School under Coach Rodger Fairless.

fastballs. A lot of these youngsters never get a shot at pro baseball because they injure their arm in the process. Maddux started out with a pitch that would not only preserve his arm but eventually make him the best pitcher in all of baseball.

Maddux learned not just a pitch, but a lot about pitching, from Ralph Medar. Maddux recalled Medar telling him to throw a high fastball and then follow it up with a pitch in the dirt. At first he could not understand being told to intentionally throw a ball instead of a strike. But then he came to realize that it was all a part of the pitching strategy. "I think that's where it really started as far as learning about pitching," Maddux said. "Coaches always want you to throw strikes. This was the first time I was ever told to throw a ball."

After graduating from Valley High School in 1984, Maddux had a decision to make. Should he go to college, getting an education while playing baseball, or should he go straight into the pros?

A few years earlier, Mike had faced a similar choice. He had been drafted by the Cincinnati Reds but decided to attend college and then enter the professional ranks. He eventually signed a contract with the Philadelphia Phillies organization and made it up to the majors in 1986.

The Maddux family placed a great deal of stock in the value of a college education. Greg had even signed a letter of intent to play baseball at the University of Arizona. It would have meant the chance to play for Jerry Kindall, one of the great college coaches of all time. Kindall is a former major-league player and is known as a great teacher, not just of baseball but of character and responsibility. The Maddux family was also impressed with Kindall's reputation of taking care of his pitchers. Some coaches are so intent on winning that they will overwork some of their star pitchers. The price of a couple extra wins can be the ruining of a pitcher's arm

Greg looked forward to playing for Jerry Kindall at the University of Arizona (shown here). Kindall is known as a great teacher of baseball, as well as of character.

and his chances of a pro career. Maddux knew Kindall was not that kind of coach and looked forward to pitching for him.

However, that never happened. After high school, Maddux was drafted by the Chicago Cubs in the second round of the amateur draft. He considered following his brother's route, attending college first. But the Cubs made Maddux such an outstanding offer that he decided to bypass college and start pro ball right away.

The Cubs' offer included an $82,000 bonus. That is a tremendous sum of money for just about anyone, let alone a young man barely eighteen years old. It was enough, Maddux knew, to allow him to go back to college and still get an education should his baseball career not work out.

Some people might spend the money foolishly. But Maddux knew the value of a dollar. He had worked a number of summer jobs while growing up, at places like a department store and a fast-food restaurant, where he flipped hamburgers. He was not about to waste his bonus money.

He put it in the bank and lived off his savings from his summer jobs as well as the small salary he started earning as a minor leaguer. He made a promise to himself that he would not dip into the bonus money until he made the majors.

It was a promise that he kept.

Chapter 3

As it turned out, Greg Maddux did not have to wait all that long to start spending his bonus money. He made a rapid rise through the minor leagues and reached the majors in just over two years.

Maddux's first stop was in Pikeville, Kentucky, pitching in the Appalachian League. He had a win-loss record of 6–2 with an earned run average of 2.63. He also had two shutouts, tying for the league lead. It was an outstanding start to his pro career. It was also a great learning experience for Maddux. Rick Kranitz, the pitching coach at Pikeville, worked with him on his change-up. Maddux altered his grip on the ball for the change-up. As a result, the spin on the pitch was almost the same as when he threw his fastball. Batters often try to figure out what kind of a pitch is coming their way by looking at the spin. Now Maddux's change-up resembled his fastball as it left his hand, making it all the tougher on the hitters.

Maddux was promoted to Peoria in the Midwest League in 1985. Once again, he got off to a great start, striking out twelve batters in the first game of the season. He won eleven of his first sixteen decisions before fading a bit and finishing the year with a record of 13–9.

Maddux continued advancing up the minor-league ladder in 1986. He began the season with Pittsfield in the Eastern League but was quickly moved up to the Iowa Cubs in the American Association, a Triple-A league just a step away from the majors. Maddux responded with an outstanding performance. In eighteen appearances with Iowa, he compiled a record of 10–1. "He's a good competitor and he's fun to watch," said Iowa pitching coach Jim Colborn of Maddux. "He's one of my favorite pitchers." Maddux finished up with a flair in Iowa. He was named the American Association's Player of the Month in August.

The Chicago Cubs—Iowa's parent team—were in need of pitching help at this time. On September 1, major-league teams are allowed to expand their rosters for the final month of the season. The Cubs took advantage of this by calling up several minor leaguers, including a couple of pitchers. Greg Maddux was one of them. Barely twenty years old, he had already made the majors. To get an idea of how remarkable this was, consider the fact that Greg's brother, Mike, had beaten him to the major leagues by only three months. Mike had been in the minors since 1982 and had pitched in college for three years previously.

Maddux felt a bit in awe as he walked into a major-league clubhouse for the first time. "Some of the guys I saw in the clubhouse when I first walked in I watched when I was ten years old. I remember watching Gary Matthews play at Dodger Stadium when I was about six years old. That's kind of nice."

Not only was Maddux barely out of his teens, he looked young for his age. In fact, Cubs' manager Gene Michael even

When Maddux was called up from the minor leagues to play for the Chicago Cubs, he looked so young the team manager mistook him for a batboy.

mistook his new pitcher for the team's batboy. Some of his teammates good-naturedly started calling him "Batboy."

One of Maddux's new teammates, pitcher Rick Sutcliffe, knew who he was, though. As Maddux was getting into his uniform for his first day in the majors, he said to Sutcliffe, "I guess I better get out there."

Sutcliffe replied, "With the kind of year you've had, you can do anything you want." The two became friends, and Sutcliffe turned into a teacher of sorts for Maddux. Years later, in a profile in *Baseball Digest,* Maddux listed Sutcliffe as "the player I learned the most from."

Greg Maddux, as usual, knew how to discover things on his own. When he was not pitching himself, he would concentrate on the pitchers who were on the mound, watching and learning.

Maddux got into his first major-league game on September 3, 1986. He was actually coming into the 18th inning of a game that had been started the day before. Chicago's Wrigley Field was the only major-league ballpark still without lights at that time. The game between the Cubs and Astros had been suspended because of darkness after fourteen innings. The game resumed the next day and remained tied into the 18th when Maddux took the mound. He retired the first batter he faced, Craig Reynolds, on a ground out. But then he gave up a home run to Billy Hatcher. The Houston Astros won the game, 8–7, and Maddux was the losing pitcher.

Even so, Gene Michael had good things to say about Maddux. "He made one mistake, but I like what I see in him." Michael also hinted that he might even give Maddux a chance to start a game. Four days later, he did just that.

The Cubs had lost seven straight games when Maddux took the hill in Cincinnati on Sunday, September 7. He ended

It was Maddux vs. Maddux in 1986, as brothers Greg and Mike (shown here) battled it out.

the team's skid by pitching a complete game and winning, 11–3, his first victory in the majors.

Maddux got another win before the season was finished, beating Philadelphia; this one was notable for a reason. The pitcher for the Phillies in this game was Mike Maddux. "I look forward to any game," said Greg afterward, "but this one was a little more fun. I had a lot more pride in getting bragging rights for the winter."

Mike took the loss in stride. "It's not the first time he's beaten me. I think our record is about .500 in whiffle ball in the backyard."

Although they were adversaries in the game, the brothers went out together after the game and celebrated the fact that they were both playing major-league baseball.

Chapter 4

In 1987, Greg Maddux did impress his team—and the fans—with his toughness and hard-nosed style of play. In a game against the Giants in late April, Chris Speier hit a line drive that nailed Maddux right below the belt buckle. Although he collapsed in pain after being hit in the groin, he got up and resumed pitching. Later in the game, he got hit by another liner, this one off his shin. To Maddux, it probably seemed harmless after the earlier shot. Once again, he stayed in and went on to win his first game of the 1987 season.

Two days later, he helped the Cubs win again, even though he was not pitching. Maddux came in as a pinch runner in the eighth inning of a tie game against the San Diego Padres. Maddux was at second, with two out, when Shawon Dunston singled to left.

Maddux was waved home but looked like he would be out at the plate when the throw from the outfield arrived ahead of him. However, Padres' catcher Benito Santiago bobbled the ball. Maddux took advantage of the opportunity. He lowered his shoulder and crashed into Santiago, causing him to drop the ball. Maddux scored the go-ahead run on the play and the Cubs won the game.

Maddux may have been a bit sore after his collision with Santiago, but he remarked, "This beats getting line drives hit at you all the time."

"He's got a heart made of gold and a wheelbarrow full of guts," said pitcher Rick Sutcliffe of Maddux. "He's not afraid of anything."

As for the rest of the Cubs, they quit calling Maddux "Batboy" and gave him a new nickname: "Mad Dog." Meanwhile, members of the press began referring to Maddux as the "Baby-faced Assassin."

But 1987 was a frustrating year for Maddux. "I had had a pretty good change-up when I was in the minors," he later explained, "but when I got to the big leagues, I had forgotten how to throw it, so I became a one-pitch pitcher. I threw just fastballs and didn't locate them very well. I spent as much time backing up the bases as I did throwing pitches."

The Cubs sent Maddux back down to Iowa in August of 1987. The pitching coach in Iowa was Dick Pole, who had been Maddux's pitching coach in Peoria the year before. Maddux had great regard for Pole, and the Cubs hoped Pole might be able to help him out.

Pole made some changes to the way Maddux gripped the ball, and it paid off right away. Maddux went 3–0 with Iowa and soon was back up with the Cubs.

After the season, Maddux had the chance to work with Pole again. Pole was the pitching coach for a winter-league team in Maracaibo, Venezuela, that Maddux pitched for. Maddux enjoyed being back with Pole, but he enjoyed his winter-league experience for another reason. His brother, Mike, was also pitching on the team. It was the first time Mike and Greg had ever been teammates.

Going into 1988, Maddux had only a total of eight major-league wins under his belt. He talked to his father during the spring. Both figured that it would be a great year if he could win eight games that season.

He knocked off half that total in the opening month alone. After beating Atlanta, 3–0, in his first start of the year, Maddux finished April with a record of 4–1 and an ERA of 2.20. He stayed hot through the first half of the season. In May, Maddux had a streak of more than twenty-six straight shutout innings over three games. The scoreless string started in a May 6 game against the Giants. Five days later, Maddux pitched a complete game shutout as the Cubs beat San Diego, 1–0, in ten innings. Maddux gave up only three hits in the game and retired the final twenty San Diego batters that he faced. The Cubs finally won the game for him by coming up with a run in the last of the 10th inning.

In his next start, he pitched another ten shutout innings, against St. Louis. But once again his teammates had trouble getting any runs for him. With two out in the 11th, Maddux lost the game when he gave up a bad-hop single to Luís Alicea of the Cardinals.

That tough-luck game was his only loss between May 1 and July 20. Maddux won all five of his decisions in June and was named National League Pitcher of the Month. On Sunday, July 10, he won his ninth-straight game to give him a record of 15–3 at the All-Star break.

If he had not just pitched, Maddux undoubtedly would have been the starting pitcher in the All-Star Game. Even so, he had captured the national baseball spotlight.

Maddux cooled off during the last half of 1988 but still finished the year with 18 wins, more than double the total he had racked up throughout his entire major-league career prior to the season.

At the beginning of the 1988 season, Maddux and his father set a goal of *eight* wins for Maddux. By the All-Star break, his win-loss record was 15–3!

His outstanding season gave him the chance to be part of a group of major leaguers who went overseas after the season to play a number of games against Japanese teams. For Maddux, there was another reason that the trip was especially thrilling. The team of all-stars was managed by Sparky Anderson, the manager of the Detroit Tigers. In the 1970s, during the time Maddux was growing up as a Cincinnati Reds' fan, Anderson was managing the Reds. He was the leader of the great "Big Red Machine" teams that won back-to-back World Series in 1975 and 1976. Maddux got a real charge out of having the chance to play for a manager he had idolized as a kid.

Maddux started the 1989 season struggling the same way he had finished up 1988. By the middle of May, his win-loss record was 1–5. His one win was a classic, though. In late April, he outdueled the Dodgers' Orel Hershiser, who had won the National League Cy Young Award the year before. The Cubs won, 1–0, as Maddux gave up only five hits and scored the game's only run.

Maddux bounced back from his rocky start and managed to have an 8–7 record at the All-Star break in July. Then he really started to regain his touch. It was a good time to get hot. The Cubs were finding themselves in a pennant race for the first time in several years. Maddux needed to be in top form.

In early August, the Cubs and Montreal Expos were tied for first place in the National League Eastern Division. The Cubs were opening a three-game series with the Expos at Wrigley Field. In the series opener, Maddux went the distance, winning 5–2, giving the Cubs sole possession of first place. Chicago went on to sweep the series with Montreal and held the top spot the rest of the way.

Seven weeks later, Maddux was on the mound again as the Cubs clinched the division title by beating the Expos in Montreal. For Maddux, it was his nineteenth win of the season. He had one more start scheduled and had a chance to win twenty games for the first time in his career.

However, he had other thoughts beyond personal glory. Cubs' manager Don Zimmer wanted Maddux to be the starting pitcher in the National League Championship Series against the San Francisco Giants. Zimmer and Maddux decided it would be better for the team if he passed up his shot for twenty wins and rested his arm for the playoffs instead.

Unfortunately, the rest did not help. Maddux was hit hard by the Giants in both games he pitched in the playoff series. The San Francisco hitters roughed up nearly all the Cubs' pitchers they faced and won the playoffs, 4 games to 1.

It had been a great season, but the ending was a letdown for Maddux, the team, and their fans. The Cubs had not been in the World Series since 1945, and Maddux had hoped to help them get there again. When it did not work out that way, Maddux called it the biggest disappointment of his career.

Maddux got off to a good start in 1990, winning four of his first five games. But then, for some reason, he hit a rocky stretch that lasted for more than two months. He went thirteen starts in a row without winning a game.

Maddux's teammate, Rick Sutcliffe, was impressed with how Maddux had dealt with the difficult period. Sutcliffe had once been told by a Hall of Fame pitcher that a pitcher cannot always control whether he wins or loses a game. Too many things can happen. But the one thing a pitcher can always control is his effort. "Greg's effort never changed," Sutcliffe said. "The effort has always been there."

Maddux never let down during his winless streak. He kept trying and it paid off. Starting in the middle of July, Maddux won five games in a row; his earned run average over those five games was well under one run per game.

Maddux was on the mound the night Chicago clinched the division title by beating the Expos in Montreal.

He rebounded to finish the season with a record of 15–15. Unfortunately, his team did not bounce back as well. After winning the division the year before, the Cubs dropped down to fifth place.

Maddux won 15 games again in 1991 and was being recognized as one of the better pitchers in the National League. He was having a good career but had not yet put it all together. He displayed brilliance on the mound at times but also went through tough times. If he was going to go from being a good pitcher to a great one, he would have to become more consistent.

Before the 1992 season, he developed a new pitch with the help of Cubs' pitching coach Billy Connors. The pitch was a "cut fastball," which has slightly less speed but more movement than a normal fastball. Although a fastball is considered a straight pitch, it still tails off as it approaches the plate—moving either towards a hitter or away from him. Hitters can often anticipate this movement and be ready for it. But a cut fastball will tail off in the opposite direction of a normal fastball.

"There are certain things you can do to a baseball to get it to move both ways," Maddux has said. "You can get it to go right-to-left or left-to-right. The hard part is to disguise it—not give it away, not have the hitter be able to see it coming."

Hitters have little enough time to react to a fastball. As it approaches the plate, they have to make a split-second decision on whether to swing or not. Then they have to get their bat around and try to make contact. When they have to try to guess which direction the ball will move as it approaches, it makes it all that much harder.

Maddux adds that another key is to have the movement on his cut fastball be as late as possible. "When you can get it to move late, in the last 10 or 15 feet in front of the plate as the ball gets closer to the hitter, it's harder to see."

Before the 1992 season, Maddux developed a new pitch called the "cut fastball" with the help of pitching coach Billy Connors.

"What he has is a lot of movement at the end of his pitch, something I call late life," said one National League pitching coach of Maddux. "His pitches will come in and have a great deal of action when they're nearing the batter. This creates a lot of frustration for hitters."

With his new pitch and its "late life," Maddux got off to a good start in 1992. He won his first three games and then faced Pittsburgh's Randy Tomlin, who was also 3–0. Maddux pitched well but lost the duel. Even though he gave up only four hits and one run, the Cubs could not score off Tomlin. The Pirates won the game, 1–0, and Maddux had his first loss of the season. In his next outing, the Cubs were once again shut out. No matter how well a pitcher pitches, he cannot win if his team does not score any runs. In the middle of May, Maddux pitched two consecutive games in which his hitters did not give him any support. His record was 4–4. In all four of his losses, the Cubs had been shut out. (Three more times during the season he would lose a game after the Cubs did not get any runs for him.)

Maddux was learning first-hand about the advice Rick Sutcliffe had once received: A pitcher cannot always control whether he wins or loses. But, as always, he did control his effort. He had ten wins by early July and was named to the National League All-Star team. It was the second time he had received the honor.

He pitched a little over an inning in relief of National League starter Tommy Glavine. Glavine, of the Atlanta Braves, had a 13–3 record at the time. Glavine had received the Cy Young Award in 1991 and seemed well on his way to winning it for the second straight year.

Maddux kept plugging away over the second half of the season. In mid-August, he shut out the Houston Astros on four hits for his fifteenth win. Maddux still had few thoughts of winning the Cy Young Award, though. A few days later, Glavine won his nineteenth game and looked like he had a lock on the honor. But Glavine would win only one more game the rest of the season.

Maddux continued to win and had a shot at a twenty-victory season for the first time in his career. The Cubs were ahead in a game at Montreal when Maddux was taken out in the seventh inning. But the Chicago bullpen blew the lead in the last of the ninth and Maddux did not get the win.

He would have one more shot at twenty wins. His final start of the season was against Pittsburgh and Randy Tomlin, who had handed Maddux his first loss of the year. But this time, it was Maddux who came out on top. He went the distance, striking out nine as he shut out the Pirates, 6–0. He was finally a twenty-game winner.

Not only that, Glavine's late season collapse opened up the Cy Young race. Maddux came out on top in that, as well. He received twenty out of twenty-four first-place votes and received the Cy Young Award.

He had finally put it all together—his great assortment of pitches combined with the pitching smarts he had acquired by being such a great student of the game.

"He knows how to pitch," said Chicago catcher Joe Girardi, referring to Maddux's knack for fooling hitters by mixing up his pitches.

"Greg has a feel for pitching and for what pitching is all about," added Cubs' general manager Larry Himes.

Chicago fans were thrilled with Maddux's season. But they were also left wondering whether Maddux would be back the following year.

His contract with the Cubs had expired, meaning that other teams could bid for his services. Greg Maddux's timing was

Greg Maddux won the 1992 Cy Young Award, receiving twenty out of twenty-four first-place votes.

good. He had become a free agent following the best season of his career.

His first choice was to stay in Chicago. “I grew up a Cub,” he said, referring to the fact that he had been with the organization for more than eight years. “That’s all I knew.” The Cubs had their chance to sign Maddux to an extended contract, but they missed the opportunity. They were undergoing changes in their management and gave up the chance to re-sign Maddux who said, “My time in Chicago was up. At least the front office felt so.”

A Cy Young Award winner was now available on the open market. There were a lot of teams in the major leagues hoping to get Maddux to pitch for them.

Chapter 5

Maddux once labeled his brother Mike the person who influenced him the most in his life. Mike and Greg have always been close, even though there is several years' difference in their ages. More than that, there is an extreme difference in their personalities.

Mike is more outgoing and likes to be around a lot of people. Greg is more shy and prefers to stay to himself. "Greg had a lot of friends, but he's always been shy around strangers," said Dave Maddux of his younger son. Greg prefers quiet surroundings and to be with just a few close friends instead of with a large group of people. "I'd rather go to a place that's not packed," he once said.

For a person like Maddux, being a big-name baseball player could be a problem. Fans usually flock around star athletes, stopping them on the street to get an autograph or coming over to talk to them in a restaurant.

But Maddux's low-key style helps him to blend in. People often walk by without realizing that they have just passed the best pitcher in baseball. During the time he played with the

Greg Maddux has said that his brother Mike (shown here) is the person who influenced him most in life.

Cubs, Maddux lived in a high-rise apartment building not far from Wrigley Field. When he would take his two Shih Tzu dogs, Sport and Slugger, out for a walk, people would pay more attention to the dogs than to the man walking them.

"Greg just doesn't stand out," says his wife, Kathy, whom he has known since high school. She adds that, "Simple things make him happy. That's just the type of person he is."

Maddux is just as laid-back when he is at home with Kathy and their daughter, Amanda, who was born in December 1993. "Greg has never changed, on the field or off the field," Kathy explains. "Whether he has a good game or a bad game, he's the same guy when he comes home."

The Madduxes always return home to Las Vegas to live when the baseball season is over. Maddux has season tickets to see the Las Vegas Thunder, a minor-league hockey team. But he is just as content staying in and doing things at home. "I just kind of like to lie around," he said. "I like to watch TV and play Nintendo™ and Turbographics™."

Maddux's one passion besides baseball and his family is golf. "There's nothing I enjoy more than making a 20-foot putt. It doesn't get any better than that."

His family claims Maddux is plenty lucky when it comes to golf and other games. His father nicknamed him "Nate Luck," and the rest of the Madduxes call him "Nate." Maddux, however, laughs and says, "I don't know where he gets that from." He reminds his dad and brother that they also get their share of lucky bounces on the golf course; they just do not take advantage of the breaks the way Greg does.

Taking advantage of good fortune also extends to the baseball diamond for Maddux. "I've caught my breaks. Everybody catches breaks but it's what you do after those breaks that will determine if it's a good break."

Although he loves golf, Maddux never loses sight of what baseball has done for him. "All the things I have are because of baseball."

Realizing the importance of baseball, Maddux takes care of himself. He has always been careful to protect his arm. A few years into his major-league career, he took it a step further by taking out an insurance policy on his arm. If he hurt it to the point that he could no longer pitch, he would at least be assured of his income continuing. "You buy insurance for your car and house," he said, "so why not for your arm or body? It's a good feeling." Maddux said that the insurance policy left him with peace of mind. Instead of being terrified of getting hurt, he could concentrate on pitching and helping his team win games.

Through the years, as Maddux's income increased, he would increase the size of the policy. By 1992 his arm was insured for $10 million.

Maddux quietly goes about his work, such as in 1995 when he pitched more than fifty-one innings without walking a batter. Although he is quiet about it, the opposition knows how good he is.

Montreal manager Felipe Alou used to play on the San Francisco Giants with pitching great Juan Marichal. "Maddux is like Marichal," said Alou. "He's got all the pitches."

St. Louis Cardinals' outfielder Ron Gant has called Maddux the "best pitcher of our time."

It has been said that Maddux is more interested in the science of pitching than in the results that he gets. It is said that he would rather give up a hit on a good pitch than get lucky and get a batter out on a bad pitch.

But he also realizes that sometimes the result is out of his control. "If you make your pitch and the batter gets a bloop hit, you can't get upset."

Maddux has insured his arm so that he need not worry about getting injured. By 1992, his arm was insured for $10 million.

There is no question that Maddux is an analytical person. When he was struggling with his pitching early in the 1990 season, he tried to figure out why. "It wasn't a physical thing. My mechanics were okay, but I wasn't executing." To help sort things out, Maddux went to a psychologist for a number of visits. "The psychologist definitely helped turn it around."

The benefits of working with a psychologist extended to more than just baseball for Maddux. "It helped in my life and on the mound. It helped me understand myself and other people a little better. And I learned to handle the wins and losses better."

Baseball is a year-round profession for Maddux. He keeps in shape over the winter by playing golf, running, riding a bike, and working with weights. "I use mostly three-pound weights while performing exercises for my shoulder," he says. Maddux must be very careful when using weights. He does not want to lose muscle elasticity. Because of this, he uses only very light weights.

He has a normal routine he goes through before each of his turns on the mound, as well. The day before a game he starts to think about the hitters he will be facing. He tries to figure out the best way to pitch to each one.

On the day of the game, he arrives at the park about a half hour before his team begins to take batting practice. He does not like to get there too early; he is afraid he might start joking around with his teammates and lose his concentration. He likes to sit quietly, relaxing and preparing for the game.

"The best day of the week is the day I'm scheduled to pitch," he says.

Maddux makes a lot of money playing baseball. He likes the things the money has provided for him and his family. But for Greg and Kathy, there are definitely things more important than money. This became clear following the 1992 season.

Maddux was a free agent and able to pick which team he wanted to play for, starting the following season.

The New York Yankees wanted Maddux pitching for them. Maddux knew the team's general manager. It was Gene Michael, Maddux's first manager with the Cubs. Michael brought Greg and Kathy to New York, giving them a tour of the city and taking them to several Broadway shows. He also drove them around the suburbs, showing them places they could live during the season. On top of that, the Yankees offered Maddux $34 million for a five-year contract.

Maddux was on the verge of becoming a Yankee. "We were going to New York," he said. "We were trying to learn the song 'New York, New York.' We were thinking about where we wanted to live, getting everything set up."

And then the Atlanta Braves called. The Braves had won the National League pennant the last two seasons but lost in the World Series each year. They already had one of the best pitching staffs and wanted Maddux to top it off.

They did not offer as much money as the Yankees. In fact, it was $6 million less. But Maddux still saw a lot of advantages in going to Atlanta instead of New York. He ended up signing a five-year contract to play with the Braves.

Maddux said that three things went into the decision he and his wife, Kathy, made to go with the Atlanta Braves. Money was the least important of the three. Where they would be living and the team's chances of winning were more important considerations.

"We knew we were going to be raising a family and felt that a place like Atlanta would be better than a great big city like New York."

Even more than where they would be living, Maddux wanted to make sure the team he played on would have a good chance of playing in the World Series. Scott Boras, Maddux's

Maddux wanted to play for a championship team so much that he signed with the Braves instead of the Yankees, who had offered him $6 million more than the Braves.

agent, explained the biggest reason they turned down the extra money offered by the Yankees. "The Atlanta Braves were the reason. Maddux wanted to have the chance to play for the world championship. The money was secondary to him achieving his true standing in baseball by competing in a World Series. That's how important winning is to Greg Maddux—a difference of $6 million."

"To have a chance to play in the World Series, I don't think you can put a price tag on that," Maddux added. "That's something only 50 people get to do a year. I remember how it was when I was a junior in high school and our team won the state championship. I remember that game just as much as I remember pitching in the playoffs in 1989 or my first day in the big leagues or pitching against my brother."

Needless to say, the Atlanta Braves were thrilled to have Maddux on their team. "Looking down the road, this is something we really needed," said Braves' manager Bobby Cox.

Maddux would join Tommy Glavine, the pitcher he had just beaten for the Cy Young Award, and two other outstanding young pitchers, Steve Avery and John Smoltz.

"With this pitching staff," Maddux said, "the Braves have the ability to win for the entire five years I'm there."

Chapter 6

Greg Maddux was the Atlanta Braves' opening day pitcher in 1993. As luck would have it, the Braves opened their season in Chicago. This meant that Maddux's first game with his new team would be against his old team.

Many of the Chicago fans were unhappy with Maddux for leaving the Cubs. They responded by booing him. It was a strange feeling for Maddux pitching against, not for, the Cubs and getting booed at Wrigley Field. On top of that, he was matched against Mike Morgan. Maddux and Morgan had been good pals when they were both with the Cubs.

Before Maddux even made his first pitch for Atlanta, his teammates had provided him with a lead. David Justice singled home a run in the top of the first and the Braves led, 1–0. It would be the only run of the game.

As Maddux stepped out of the dugout to take the mound in the bottom of the first, the fans booed loudly. Every time he came to bat in the game, he was booed. Maddux carried his shutout into the ninth inning but needed relief help to finish it

Maddux's first game as a Brave was in Chicago against his former team, the Cubs. As a result, Maddux was booed every time he came to bat.

up. When he was taken out, the fans stood and booed as loudly as they had throughout the game.

After the game, Maddux said he was not bothered by the fans' reaction to him. "I'm just glad we won," he said, adding that he was happy his good friend Morgan had pitched a good game as well. He also said that, in some ways, the booing helped him. "Every now and then you have to remind yourself not to let up. I didn't have that problem today. The crowd did it for me."

Maddux had pitched a great game his first time out with the Braves but then struggled over the first half of the season. His record was 8–8 at the All-Star break. Atlanta fans were expecting much more from him. They were also expecting more from their team. The Braves were in second place, nine games behind the San Francisco Giants.

But Maddux won his first four games after the All-Star break, and the Braves started to chip away at the Giants' lead. In late August, the Braves went to San Francisco for a three-game series with the Giants. After watching Atlanta win the first two games, Maddux pitched the final game of the series. He gave up just one run in winning his fifteenth game of the season. By sweeping the series, the Braves had pulled within four and a half games of the Giants.

A week later, the Giants came to Atlanta. Maddux pitched the series opener. He went the distance, pitching a six-hitter to win the game. The Braves were in the hunt.

It turned out to be a great pennant race. Both teams continued to win games but the Braves managed to edge out the Giants on the final day of the season to win the National League Western Division championship. Maddux had won his twentieth game of the season the day before. After the slow start, he won thirteen of his last fifteen decisions and was a big reason why the Braves had been able to come back and win the division title.

Maddux now had another shot at getting to the World Series. The Braves would play the Philadelphia Phillies in the National League Championship Series. The Phillies won the first game, but the Braves tied the series as Maddux pitched a strong game.

Philadelphia then won two of the next three games and were within a game of going to the World Series. The Braves sent Maddux to the mound in Game Six, hoping he could keep the series going. In the first inning, Mickey Morandini of the Phillies hit a hard shot off Maddux's leg. Maddux stayed in the game but had a deep calf bruise. He would not use the injury as an excuse, but it seemed to affect him. He gave up six runs and the Phillies won the game, 6–3.

It was still a great season for Maddux, and for the second straight year he won the Cy Young Award. But he would have rather gone to the World Series. That was his goal, and one he would keep working towards.

No one had the chance to play in the World Series in 1994. The players' strike that started in August wiped out the rest of the season, including the playoffs and World Series.

The strike extended into 1995, causing the season to start three weeks late. It also looked like Maddux might miss the opening of the season when he ended up catching the chicken pox a week before the first game.

But he was still on the mound for the season opener, against the Giants. He took a no-hitter into the fifth inning, before giving up a home run. He was taken out after five innings, but was the winning pitcher in the game. In his next start, he took a no-hitter into the sixth before giving up three hits and a run. He beat the Florida Marlins for his second win.

Pitching for the Braves, Maddux won his second Cy Young Award in 1993.

In mid-May he was hit hard and lost a game to the Colorado Rockies. It was the last time hitters had any success against Maddux for quite a while. He came off his bad game with a great performance against St. Louis, once again taking a no-hitter into the sixth inning.

He went even further in his next start in Houston against the Astros. He had a no-hitter until Jeff Bagwell homered in the eighth inning. Maddux still ended up with a 3–1 win and his first career one-hitter.

Maddux was not only tough to hit against, he was tough to draw a walk from. Starting in early June and extending into mid-July, Maddux had a streak of fifty-one consecutive innings without issuing a base on balls. He won ten straight games between May and August before losing a game at home against Cincinnati.

On the road, he was unbeatable. Going into an August 26 game at Wrigley Field in Chicago, Maddux had won fifteen road decisions in a row. A win against the Cubs would break the National League record and tie the major-league record for consecutive road victories.

Maddux pitched the entire game and, in typical fashion, did not give up a walk. In this game, however, his control was truly magnificent. He did not even reach a three-ball count on any of the batters as he set a new league record with his sixteenth-straight road victory. He extended the streak to eighteen straight through the end of the season.

Maddux finished the regular season with a record of 19 wins and 2 losses. His earned run average was 1.63. There was no doubt who the Cy Young Award winner would be again in the National League. In fact, by the end of the season, Maddux was being hailed as the best right-handed pitcher in the majors in more than seventy-five years.

What Maddux was more concerned about was getting the chance to pitch in the World Series. The Braves had finished the regular season with the best record in the National League. However, they would have to win two rounds of playoffs to advance to the World Series. In previous postseason opportunities, Maddux had not pitched well, and some people wondered if he could win when the pressure was on.

Atlanta had little trouble getting by the Colorado Rockies in the opening playoff round. Maddux pitched two games in the series. He did not receive a decision in the first game even though the Braves won. He did get the win a few days later as the Braves finished off the Rockies in the series.

The Braves then faced the Cincinnati Reds in the National League Championship series. Maddux pitched the third game of that series and was outstanding. He got the win, which gave the Braves a commanding lead in the series. Atlanta won the next game to win the National League pennant and advance to the World Series.

Since the Braves had swept their series against the Reds, they would have nearly a week off before the World Series started. Maddux was well rested as he took the mound for the first game of the series against the Cleveland Indians, the best hitting team in the major leagues in 1995.

With the spotlight on him, Maddux performed brilliantly. He allowed only three baserunners all night—two on singles and one on an error—as the Braves beat the Indians, 3–2. Cleveland coach Buddy Bell said afterward, "That was the best pitched game I have ever seen. I don't know how you can be more perfect."

As for Greg Maddux, he called it "my best game ever, all things considered."

The Braves won two of the next three games and had the chance to finish off the Indians with Maddux on the mound in

Greg Maddux has been hailed as the best right-handed pitcher in the majors in more than seventy-five years.

Game Five. Things did not go as well for Maddux in this one, and the Indians won it. Even so, the Braves won the next game and, with it, the World Series.

The awards flowed in after the season. Maddux received the Cy Young Award for the fourth consecutive year. No pitcher had ever before won even three straight Cy Young Awards, let alone four. For the second year in a row, no other National League pitcher besides Maddux even received a first-place vote in the balloting. Maddux also received a Gold Glove as the best fielding pitcher in the National League for the sixth straight year.

On top of that, Maddux was named the Associated Press Player of the Year for 1995. This award covered both the National and American Leagues. It meant that Maddux was being recognized as the best player in the major leagues. It was also the first time a pitcher had received this honor.

But individual awards were getting to be old hat for Greg Maddux. In 1995 he had something more meaningful to celebrate: a world championship. Maddux was more proud of the title he had helped his team win than any honor he received personally.

"It's all about winning," Maddux said, "to make every effort possible to win—for your team, for your city, for your teammates."

For the first time in his career, Greg Maddux was a member of a world championship team. And, to him, that is what it is all about.

Career Statistics

Year	Team	W	L	ERA	G	GS	CG	ShO	IP	BB	SO
1986	Chicago	2	4	5.52	6	5	1	0	31.0	11	20
1987	Chicago	6	14	5.61	30	27	1	1	155.6	74	101
1988	Chicago	18	8	3.18	34	34	9	3	249.0	81	140
1989	Chicago	19	12	2.95	35	35	7	1	238.3	82	135
1990	Chicago	15	15	3.46	35	35	8	2	237.0	71	144
1991	Chicago	15	11	3.35	37	37	7	2	263.0	66	198
1992	Chicago	20	11	2.18	35	35	9	4	268.0	70	199
1993	Atlanta	20	10	2.36	36	36	8	1	267.0	52	197
1994	Atlanta	16	6	1.56	25	25	10	3	202.0	31	156
1995	Atlanta	19	2	1.63	28	28	10	3	209.6	23	181
Totals		150	93	2.88	301	297	70	20	2,120.5	561	1,471

WORLD SERIES										
Year	W	L	ERA	G	GS	CG	ShO	IP	BB	SO
1995	1	1	2.25	2	2	1	0	16	3	8

W=wins
L=losses
ERA=earned run average
G=games pitched
GS=games started
CG=complete games
ShO=shutouts
IP=innings pitched
BB=bases on ball (walks)
SO=strikeouts

Where to Write to Greg Maddux:

Mr. Greg Maddux
Atlanta Braves
Centennial Olympic Stadium
Box 4064
Atlanta, GA 30302

Index